I0527346

Henry Sidgwick

The Scope and Method of Economic Science

Henry Sidgwick

The Scope and Method of Economic Science

ISBN/EAN: 9783337033781

Printed in Europe, USA, Canada, Australia, Japan

Cover: Foto ©Suzi / pixelio.de

More available books at **www.hansebooks.com**

THE SCOPE AND METHOD OF ECONOMIC SCIENCE.

An Address

DELIVERED TO THE ECONOMIC SCIENCE AND
STATISTICS SECTION OF THE BRITISH
ASSOCIATION AT ABERDEEN

10 SEPTEMBER, 1885.

BY

PROF. HENRY SIDGWICK, M.A., Litt.D.

PRESIDENT OF THE SECTION.

London:

MACMILLAN AND CO.

1885

[All Rights reserved.]

𝕮𝖆𝖒𝖇𝖗𝖎𝖉𝖌𝖊 :

PRINTED BY C. J. CLAY, M.A. AND SON,

AT THE UNIVERSITY PRESS.

I HAVE chosen for the subject of the discourse, which by custom has to be delivered from the chair that I am called upon to occupy, the scope and method of economic science, and its relation to other departments of what is vaguely called 'social science.' If the abstract and academic nature of the subject, together with my own deficiencies as an expositor, should render my remarks less interesting to the audience than they have a right to expect, I trust that they will give me what indulgence they can; but, above all, that they will not anticipate a corresponding remoteness from concrete fact in the discussions that are to follow. I see from the records of the Association that it has been the custom in this department—and it seems to me a good custom—to give to the annual addresses of the presidents the variety that naturally

S.   1

results when each speaker in turn applies himself unreservedly to that aspect of our complex and many-sided inquiry which his special studies and opportunities have best qualified him to treat; and as my own connection with economic science has been in the way of studying, criticising, and developing theories, rather than collecting and systematising facts, I have thought that I should at any rate have a greater chance of making a useful contribution to our discussions if I allowed myself to deal with the subject from the point of view that is most familiar to me.

I have the less scruple in adopting this course because I do not think that any who may listen to my remarks are likely to charge me with overrating the value of abstract reasoning on economic subjects, or regarding it as a substitute for an accurate and thorough investigation of facts instead of an indispensable instrument of such investigation. There is indeed a kind of political economy which flourishes in proud independence of facts; and undertakes to settle all practical problems of Governmental interference or private philanthropy by simple deduction from one or two general assumptions—of which the chief is the assumption of the universally beneficent and harmonious operation of self-interest well let alone. This kind of political economy is sometimes called 'orthodox,' though it has the characteristic unusual in orthodox doctrines of being repudiated by the majority of accredited teachers of the subject. But whether orthodox or not, I must be allowed to disclaim all connection with it; the more completely this survival of the *à priori* politics of the eighteenth century can be banished to the remotest available planet, the better it will be, in my opinion, for the progress of economic science. Since, however, this kind of political economy is still somewhat current in the market-place, since the language of newspapers and public speakers still keeps up the impression that the professor of political economy is continually laying down laws which practical people are continually violating, it seems worth while to try to make clear the relation between the economic science which we are concerned to study and the

1—2

principles of Governmental interference—or rather
non-interference—which are thought to have been
of late so persistently and in some cases so success-
fully outraged.

It must be admitted at once that there is considerable excuse for the popular misapprehension
just mentioned; since for more than a century the
general interest taken in the analysis of the phenomena of industry has been mainly due to the
connection of this analysis with a political movement
towards greater industrial freedom. No researches
into the historical development of economic studies
before Adam Smith can displace the great Scotch-
man from his position as the founder of modern
political economy considered as an independent
science, with a well-marked field of investigation
and a definite and characteristic method of reasoning.
And no doubt the element of Adam Smith's treatise
which makes the most impression on the ordinary
reader is his forcible advocacy of the 'system of
natural liberty;' his exposition of the natural
'division of labour'—tending, if left alone, to be-

come an international division of employments—as
the main cause of the 'universal opulence' of 'well-
governed' societies; and of the manner in which, in
this distribution of employments, individual capitalists seeking their own advantage are led 'by an
invisible hand' to 'prefer that employment of their
capital which is most advantageous to society.'

At the same time Adam Smith was too cool and
too shrewd an observer of facts to be carried, even
by the force and persuasiveness of his own arguments, into a sweeping and unqualified assertion
of the universality of the tendency that he describes.
His advocacy of natural liberty in no way blinds
him to the perpetual and complex opposition and
conflict of economic interests involved in the un-
fettered efforts of individuals to get rich. He even
goes the length of saying that 'the interest of the
dealers in any particular branch of trade or manu-
facture is always in some respects different from,
and even opposite to, that of the public.' To take
a particular case, he is decidedly of opinion that
the natural liberty of bankers to issue notes may

reasonably be restrained by the laws of the freest Governments. He is quite aware, again, that the absence of Governmental interference does not necessarily imply a state of free competition, since the self-interest of individuals may lead them, on the contrary, to restrict competition by 'voluntary associations and agreements.' He does not doubt that Governments, central or local, may find various ways of employing wealth—of which elementary education is one of the most important—which will be even economically advantageous to society, though they could not be remuneratively undertaken by individual capitalists. In short, however fascinating the picture that Adam Smith presents to us of the continual and complex play of individual interests constituting and regulating the vast fabric of social industry, the summary conclusion drawn by some of his disciples that the social production of wealth will always be best promoted by leaving it altogether alone, that the only petition which industry should make to Government is the petition of Diogenes to Alexander that he would cease to stand between

him and the sunshine, and that statesmen are therefore relieved from the necessity of examining carefully
the grounds for industrial intervention in any particular case—this comfortable and labour-saving
conclusion finds no support in a fair survey of Adam
Smith's reasonings, though it has been no doubt
encouraged by some of his phrases. To attribute to
him a dogmatic theory of the natural right of the
individual to absolute industrial independence—as
some recent German writers are disposed to do[1]—is
to construct the history of economic doctrines from
one's inner consciousness.

It is true, as I have said, that among Adam
Smith's disciples there were not a few who rushed
to the sweeping generalisations that the master had
avoided. In England, in particular, the influence of
the more abstract and purely deductive method of
Ricardo tended in this direction. It was natural,
again, that in the heat of a political movement

---

[1] *E.g.* v. Scheel, in Schönberg's *Handbuch der politischen
Oekonomie*, p. 89, speaks of 'Die naturrechtliche Wirthschafts-
theorie oder der Smithianismus.'

absolute and unqualified statements of principle should come into vogue, since the ease and simplicity with which they can be enunciated and apprehended makes them more effective instruments of popular agitation : hence it is not surprising to find the anti-corn-law petitions declaring the 'inalienable right of every man freely to exchange the result of his labour for the productions of other people,' to be 'one of the principles of eternal justice.' But under the more philosophic guidance of J. S. Mill, English political economy shook off all connection with these antiquated metaphysics, and during the last generation has been generally united with a view of political principles more balanced, qualified, and empirical, and therefore more in harmony with the general tendencies of modern scientific thought.

If, indeed, *laisser-faire* were—as many suppose—the one main doctrine of modern political economy, there can be no doubt that the decisive step forward that founded the science ought to be attributed not to Adam Smith, but to his French predecessors the 'Physiocrats.' It is to them—to Quesnay, De

Gournay, De la Rivière, Turgot—that the credit, whatever it may be, is due of having first proclaimed to the world with the utmost generality and without qualification that what a statesman had to do was not to make laws for industry, but merely to ascertain and protect from encroachment the simple, eternal, and immutable laws of nature, under which ✗ the production of wealth would regulate itself in the best possible way if men would abstain from meddling.

This doctrine formed one part of the impetuous movement of thought against the existing political order which characterised French speculation during the forty years that preceded the great Revolution. It was, we may say, the counterpart and complement of the doctrine of which Rousseau was the chief prophet. The sect of the Économistes and the disciples of Rousseau were agreed that the existing political system needed radical change; and in both there was a tendency to believe that an ideal political order could at once be constituted. At this point, however, their courses diverged: the school of Rousseau held that the essential thing was to alter the *structure* of government, and to keep legislation effectually in the hands of the sovereign people; the Économistes thought that the all-important point was to limit the *functions* of government, holding that the simple duty of maintaining the natural rights of the individual to liberty and property could be best performed by an absolute monarch. Both movements had much justification; both have had effects on the political and social life of Europe of which it is difficult to measure the extent; but both doctrines—attained, as they were, by a fallacious method—involved a large element of exaggeration, suitable to the ardent and sanguine period that brought them forth, but which gives them a curious air of absurdity when they are resuscitated and offered for the acceptance of our more sober, circumspect, and empirically-minded age. In the most civilised countries of Europe it is now a recognised and established safeguard against oppressive laws that an effective control over legislation is vested in the people at large; but no serious thinker would now maintain with Rousseau that the predominance of the will of the sovereign people has a necessary tendency to produce just legislation. Similarly, the doctrine of the Physiocrats has prevailed, in the main, as regards the internal conditions of national industry in modern civilised societies. The old hampering privileges, restraints, and prohibitions have been almost entirely swept away, to the great advantage of the community; but the absolute right of the individual to unlimited industrial freedom is now only maintained by a scanty and dwindling handful of doctrinaires, whom the progress of economic science has left stranded on the crude generalisations of an earlier period.

There will probably always be considerable disagreement in details among competent persons as to the propriety of Governmental interference in particular cases; but, apart from questions on which economic considerations must yield to political, moral, or social reasons of greater importance, it is an anachronism not to recognise fully and frankly the existence of cases in which the industrial intervention of Government is desirable, even with a view to the most economical production of wealth. Hence, I conceive, the present business of economic theory in this department is to give a systematic and carefully-reasoned exposition of these cases, which, until the constitution of human nature and society are fundamentally altered, must always be regarded as exceptions to a general rule of non-interference. The statesman's decision on any particular case it does not belong to abstract theory to give; this can only be rationally arrived at after a careful examination of the special conditions of each practical problem at the particular time and place at which it presents itself. But abstract reasoning may supply a systematic view of the general occasions for Governmental interference, the different possible modes of such interference, and the general reasons for and against each of them, which may aid practical men both in finding and in estimating the decisive considerations in particular cases. Thus it may show, on the one hand, under what circumstances the inevitable drawbacks of Governmental management are likely to be least, and by what methods they may be minimised; and where, on the other hand, private enterprise is likely to fail in supplying a social need—as where an undertaking socially useful is likely for various reasons to be unremunerative to the undertakers—or where private interests are liable to be markedly opposed to those of the public, as is generally the case with businesses that tend to become monopolies.

It would be tedious now to dwell at more length on these generalities; but there is one special exception to the triumph of the system of natural liberty in the civilised countries of Europe which has too much historical importance to be passed over without a word in this connection. As we are all aware, this triumph has only been decided as regards the *internal* conditions of industry and trade; the practice of imposing barriers on *international* exchange, with a view to the protection of native industry, still flourishes in the most advanced communities, and shows no immediate tendency to come to an end. It is not, I conceive, reasonable to attribute this result entirely, as some Free-traders are disposed to do, to the incapacity of mankind to understand elementary economic truths, and the interested efforts of a combination of producers to prey in a comfortable and legal way on the resources of the confiding consumers. I do not deny that both these causes have operated; but, in view of the evident ability and disinterestedness of many of the writers and statesmen who have supported the cause of Protection on the Continent or in the United States, I cannot find in them an adequate explanation of the phenomenon.

A part of the required explanation is, I think, suggested when we examine the arguments by which Free-trade was actually recommended to intelligent Englishmen at the time when England's policy was taking the decisive turn in this direction, and imagine their effect on the mind of an intelligent foreigner. Suppose, for instance, that the intelligent foreigner is studying the *Edinburgh Review* in 1841, when it came forward as a vigorous and decided advocate of Free-trade. In the January number he would find

the cosmopolitan and abstract argument with which
we are so familiar; he would learn how, under Free-
trade, 'every country will exert itself in the way
that is most beneficial in the production of wealth;'
how labour and capital will be employed in each
country to produce those things which the varieties
of climate, situation, and soil enable it to produce
with greater advantage than other countries, so that
'the greatest possible amount of industry will be
kept constantly in action, and all commodities will
exist in the greatest abundance.' But in the July
number of the same organ he would find a recom-
mendation of Free-trade from a national point of
view, which, though more restricted in its scope,
would appear to contain matter no less important
for practical consideration. He would find that the
immediate introduction of Free-trade was held to be
essential in order to keep what remained of the
manufacturing and commercial supremacy of England.
He would learn that 'the early progress of any nation
that attempts to rival us in manufactures must be
slow;' for 'it has to contend with our great capital,

our traditionary skill, our almost infinite division of labour, our long-established perseverance, energy, and enterprise, our knowledge of markets, and with the habits of those who have been bred up to be our customers.' He would learn that there was 'no reason to believe that,' in the 'absence of disturbing causes,' we should ever lose our present command of the world's market; that we might have preserved our superiority for centuries; but that 'if these difficulties were once surmounted, this superiority— so far at least as respects the commodity in which we find ourselves undersold—would be gone for ever,' in consequence of 'the well-known law of manufacturing industry that, *ceteris paribus*, with every increase of the quantity produced, the relative cost of production is diminished.' It cannot be denied that a consideration of this law, and of the *vis inertiæ* here attributed to an established superiority in manufactures and commerce, supplies an important qualification of the general argument for Free-trade. For, along with the tendency of industry to go where it can be most economically carried on,

we have also to recognise a tendency for it to stay
and develop where it has been once planted; and
the advantage of leaving this latter tendency un-
disturbed would naturally be less clear to the
patriotic foreigner than to the patriotic Englishman.
The proclamation of a free race for all, just when
England had a start which she might probably keep
'for centuries,' would not seem to him a manifest
realisation of eternal justice; to delay the race for a
generation or two, and meanwhile to apply judiciously
'disturbing causes' in the form of protective duties,
would seem likely to secure a fairer start for other
nations, and ultimately, therefore, a better organisation of the world's industry even from a cosmopolitan
point of view.

Nor would it seem to him a conclusive argument
against this course that protective duties impose
great present pecuniary sacrifices on the protecting
nation; especially when he learnt, from an impartial
English source, of the great sacrifices which private
capitalists in England were in the habit of making
to assist the tendency of free competition in their

S.   2

favour. He would find, for instance, in the Report of a Commission published in 1854[1], an appeal to the working classes to consider 'the immense losses which their employers voluntarily incur in bad times, in order to destroy foreign competition, and to gain and keep possession of foreign markets.' Should the efforts of Trade-Unionists, urges the writer, be successful for any length of time, they would interfere with the 'great accumulations of capital which enable a few of the most wealthy capitalists to overwhelm all foreign competition in times of great depression,' and which thus constitute 'the great instruments of warfare against the competing capital of foreign countries.' If it was the view of shrewd English men of business that these great sacrifices of private wealth were needed, and were worth making, to maintain the industrial start once gained, the intelligent foreigner would naturally conclude that the other combatants in the industrial battle must

[1] See p. 20 of Report by Mr H. S. Tremenheere, Commissioner appointed to inquire into the operation of Act 5 & 6 Vict. c. 99, and into the state of the population in the mining districts (Vol. XIX. of Parl. Papers for 1854).

be prepared to make corresponding sacrifices; that each nation must fight with its own weapons; and that where there were no great accumulations of capital in private hands, the instruments of warfare must be obtained by a general contribution.

I have given these considerations, not because I agree with the practical conclusion which they tend to support, but because I think that they require to be met by a line of argument different from that which English economists have usually adopted. I think it erroneous to maintain, on the ordinary economic grounds, that temporary Protection must always be detrimental to the protecting country, even if it were carried out by a perfectly wise and strong Government, able to resist all influences of sinister and sectarian interests, and to act solely for the good of the nation. The decisive argument against it is rather the political consideration that no actual Government is competent for this difficult and delicate task; that Protection, as actually applied under the play of political forces, is sure to foster many weak industries that have no chance of living with-

2 — 2

out artificial support, and to hamper industries that
might thrive independently, by the artificial dearness
of some of their materials and instruments; so that
it turns out a dangerous and clumsy, as well as a
costly, instrument of industrial competition, and is
not likely on the whole to bring the desired victory,
though it may give a partial success here and there.
And some such conclusion as this is, I think, now
prevalent even among those German economists who
are most decided in their rejection of the claims of
laisser-faire to absolute and unqualified validity.

So far I have been speaking of the function of
economic science in determining principles of Governmental intervention in matters of industry, because
this is the function prominent in the popular view of
political economy. But I need hardly say to the
present audience that this is not the view that
English economists generally have taken as to their
primary business. Indeed, during the last generation our leading economists—even those who come
nearest to the so-called 'orthodox' type—have gone
even further than I should myself go in declaring that

economic science had nothing to do with the doctrine of *laisser-faire*. No one (*e.g.*) has stated this more strongly than Cairnes, whom I select as a conspicuous and effective advocate of Free-trade. 'The maxim of *laissez-faire*,' he says, 'has no scientific basis whatever;' it is a 'mere handy rule of practice,' though 'a rule in the main sound.' According to this view, the 'laws' with which economic science is primarily concerned are the laws that determine economic quantities—the amount of the aggregate of wealth, its annual increase, the relative values of its different elements, and the shares of the economic classes that have combined to produce it—as they would be apart from special Governmental interference; and not the rules for deciding when and how far such interference is justifiable.

And it is the additional light that Adam Smith threw on the general determination of such economic quantities—and not his advocacy of natural liberty—which in the view of economists constitutes his chief claim to his place in the historical development of economic science. And I may observe that, from

this point of view, the important predecessors of
Adam Smith are not the Physiocrats only, but even
more Cantillon, who wrote a generation before, to
whom Jevons drew attention some years ago in a
remarkable essay ; nor should we overlook his English
predecessors of a still earlier age such as Petty and
Locke—the former of whom has a special interest for
us as a pioneer in each of the two lines of investigation of which we here maintain the union, since he
was the first in England to combine a serious effort
to establish the general relations of economic quantities by abstract reasoning and analysis with patient
endeavours to ascertain particular economic facts by
statistical inquiries. When we trace the gradual
evolution of the modern economic view as to the
manner in which the play of individual self-interests
tends to determine prices and shares—from the rude
beginnings of Petty and Locke, through the more
systematic and penetrating theory of Cantillon, the
fuller analysis and exposition of Adam Smith, and
the closer reasoning of Ricardo, down to the important rectifications and additions of Jevons—we see

clearly that the progress of the theory has no necessary connection with any doctrine as to the limits of the industrial intervention of Government.

And it is to be observed that neither Adam Smith nor the predecessors to whom I have referred had any design of maintaining that the distribution which they were endeavouring to analyse satisfied either the claims of ideal equity by giving each individual his deserts, or the claims of expediency by giving him what was most conducive to general happiness. Nor, since Adam Smith, has any leading English economist maintained the former of these propositions; and so far as the school of Ricardo may have seemed to maintain the latter—so far as they certainly have taught that direct Governmental interference with distribution was undesirable—it has not been from any prevalence among them of the shallow optimism of Bastiat and his followers. It is pessimism rather than optimism which is to be laid to their charge; not a disposition to underrate or ignore the hardships that the 'natural' rate of wages might entail; but a conviction that, however bad things might be naturally, the direct interference of Government could only make them worse. I am not arguing that they did not go too far in this view; I am now chiefly desirous to remove a profound and widespread misunderstanding as to the general aim and drift of their investigations, which I find in certain German and other Continental critics of English political economy,—and, I may add, in certain English critics who repeat the foreign objections. Such critics either fail to see, or continually forget, that the English economist, in giving an explanation of the manner in which prices, wages, profits, &c., are determined, is not attempting to justify the result; he is not trying to show that in getting the market price of his services the labourer, capitalist, or landlord gets what he deserves. Thus when Senior called interest the 'reward of abstinence,' he did not mean to imply that it was normally proportioned to the capitalist's merit in abstaining, but merely that capital is increased by individuals saving instead of spending, and that they require the inducement given by the actual rate of interest to save to the extent to which they actually are saving. Whether any other rate of interest would be *juster* is a question of ideal politics to which the English economist has usually nothing to say so long as it is stated in this abstract form ; it is only when the political idealist descends to practice, and proposes a scheme for realising his conception of justice, that it comes within the province of economic science to discuss the probable effects of this scheme on production and distribution. But it is not with such far-reaching proposals of change that the English economist is mainly concerned; his primary business is to ascertain the causes which determine actual prices of products and services.

Hence, when the most recent German school of economists—variously known as the 'historical,' 'ethical,' or 'social' school—claims to have moralised political economy by throwing over the assumption of egoism, which they regard as characteristic of 'Smithianismus,' they usually appear to the English economist to confound what is with what ought to be. The assumption that egoism ought to be universal—that the universal prevalence of self-interest leads necessarily to the best possible economic order—has never been made by leading English writers; and it is an assumption with which they generally conceive themselves in no way concerned—in that part, at least, of the science which deals with distribution. It is the actual prevalence of self-interest in ordinary exchanges of products and services which constitutes their fundamental assumption.

But I admit that this reply does not end the controversy. The critic may rejoin that, if egoism is not what it ought to be, the tranquil way in which the economist treats it as universally predominant is objectionable, as tending to give dangerous encouragement to the baser side of human nature. And, secondly, he may deny that self-interest actually has any such predominance as English economists assume; hence, he may argue, their fundamental assumption must lead to serious errors in the analysis and forecast of actual facts.

The first of these points I should concede to some extent. If we regarded it as blameworthy that a man should, under ordinary circumstances, try to get the highest price for any commodity he sells, and give the lowest for what he buys, then, though the analysis of economic facts, as they exist in the present selfish and wicked world, might still be conducted on the present method, I certainly think its results ought to be—and would be—expounded in a different tone. I should say, therefore, that our economists generally do not hold to be censurable, in a broad and general way, the self-regard which they assume as normal. I conceive, however, that this view is commonly held with the following important qualifications.

Firstly, it is not implied that the right of free exchange ought not to be legally limited in respect of certain special commodities. Thus, when it is urged by statesmen or philanthropists that the sale of opium, or brandy, or lottery-tickets, or children's labour ought to be prohibited or placed under certain restrictions, the political economist, as such, is not to be regarded as holding a brief on the other side—at most he only throws the *onus probandi* on those who advocate interference, adding perhaps a warning that the consequences of their measure may possibly be different from what they anticipate, owing to the play of ordinary self-regard working under the new conditions that they aim at imposing.

Secondly, it is not implied that similar limitations may not be effectively imposed by the force of moral opinion. It has, indeed, to be pointed out that morality, like law, may produce effects other than what are designed—*e.g.* that the discredit attaching to usury may cause the unhappy debtor to pay more instead of less for his inevitable loan, since the usurer has to be compensated for the social drawbacks of his despised employment. But it does not follow that there are no cases in which this disadvantage has to be faced as the least of two evils.

Thirdly, the economist does not assume that his economic man is *always* buying in the cheapest and selling in the dearest market, and never rendering services to his fellow-creatures on any other terms. He does not lay down that the economic distribution which it is his business to analyse will not be

supplemented to an indefinite extent by a distribution prompted by other motives :—indeed, it should
be noted that the ordinary economic man is always
understood to be busily providing for a wife and
children ; so that his dominant motive to industry
is rather domestic interest than self-interest, strictly
so-called. And it has never been supposed that
outside his private business—or even in connection
with it if occasion arises—a man will not spend
labour and money for public objects, and give freely
gratuitous services to friends, benefactors, and persons
in special need or distress.

The political economists, it is true, have often
felt called upon to criticise the proceedings of
philanthropists; but those who have assumed in
enunciating these criticisms a grave air of giving the
results of abstruse scientific reasoning are partly to
blame, I think, for having drawn on political economy
a kind of odium which ought to have been thrown
on the broader back of plain common sense. We
may say, indeed, with special force of a great part
of economic science what Huxley has said of science

generally—that it is only ‘organised common sense.’
But it needs little organisation to show that the
motives to industry and thrift are impaired by the
indiscriminate relief of the idle and improvident;
that you help men best by encouraging them to
help themselves, by widening the opportunities for
the display of energetic activity and enterprise, and
diffusing the knowledge that will save it from being
wasted, rather than by diminishing the inducements
that stimulate it. To apprehend the truth of propositions like these, a man need not even have read
a shilling handbook; and yet these commonplaces
constitute the greater part of the ‘hard-hearted
economist's’ criticism of sentimental philanthropy.
If, indeed, the economist has gone on to say that
therefore no efforts ought to be made to relieve distress, and raise those who have temporarily stumbled
in the struggle for existence, or if he has prophesied
failure to all larger attempts on the part of philanthropists, to improve the condition of the classes
at the base of the industrial pyramid—if, I say, an
individual economist has here and there been

found lecturing and prognosticating in this sweeping manner, he has only exemplified the common human tendency to dogmatise beyond the limits of his knowledge; and I trust the blame will not be laid on the science whose exacter methods he has deserted or misapplied.

The important question of method, then, at issue between the English economists and their German critics is not whether the play of the ordinary motives of self-interest ought to be limited and supplemented by the operation of other motives; but whether these other motives actually do, or can reasonably be expected to, operate in such a way as to destroy the general applicability of the method of economic analysis which assumes that each party to any free exchange will prefer his own interest to that of the other party. And in speaking of the German historical school as antagonists on this question, I ought to say that I refer only to what I may call their more aggressive left wing. With the more moderate claims of the historical method as set forth by the distinguished leader of the school, William Roscher,

the English economists who maintain the tradition
of Adam Smith and Ricardo have no sort of quarrel;
and Roscher expressly disclaims any quarrel with
them. He has sought, as he says, 'gratefully to
avail himself' of the results of Ricardian analysis,
and we can no less gratefully profit by the abundant
historical researches that he has led and stimulated.
It is no doubt true that our older economists often
had an insufficient appreciation of the historical
variations in economic conditions; and, in particular,
did not adequately recognise the greater extent to
which competition was limited or repressed by law or
custom in states of society economically less advanced
than our own. But for a generation there has been
no serious dispute about this; nor has there ever been
any fundamental disagreement between Ricardians
and Roscherians as to the right method of studying
the history of economic facts. The most deductive
English Economist has never gone so far as to
maintain that this can be constructed *à priori*, any
more than any other history; and if a generation ago
he was sometimes wont to dogmatise with insufficient

information as to the causes of industrial changes and the economic effects of political measures in other ages and countries, he has grown wiser, like other persons, through the great development of historical study—and of what I may call the common historic sense of educated persons—which has taken place in the interval. Indeed, I think the danger now is rather that we should go into the opposite extreme, and not give sufficient attention to the more latent and complicated but very effective manner in which competition is found operating even in states of society where the barriers of custom are strongest.

But further, even as regards the present condition of industry in the more advanced countries, to which the theory of modern economic science primarily relates, there is, I conceive, no dispute as to the need of what is called a 'realistic' or 'inductive' method—*i.e.* as to the need of accurately ascertaining particular facts when we are inquiring into the particular causes of particular values, or of the shares of particular economic classes at any given

S.   3

place and time. All that the deductive reasonings of English economists supply is a method of analysing the phenomena and a statement of the general causes that govern them, and of the manner of their operation. In this analysis, no doubt, the assumption is fundamental that the individuals concerned in the actual determination of the economic quantities resulting from free exchange will aim, *ceteris paribus*, at getting the most they can for what they sell and giving the least they can for what they buy. And when we find the legitimacy of this assumption, and the scientific value of the analysis based upon it, broadly assailed by Hildebrand[1], Knies[2], and others, we are no doubt seriously concerned to meet their criticism.

For my own part, I can only say that, having searched their works with the interest and respect

---

[1] See two papers on 'Die gegenwärtige Aufgabe der Wissenschaft der politischen Oekonomie,' in the first volume (1863) of Hildebrand's *Jahrbuch für National-Oekonomie u. Statistik*, p. 5ff. and p. 137ff.: especially his criticism of J. S. Mill (p. 23), quoted with approval by Schönberg in the introduction to his *Handbuch*.

[2] See his *Politische Oekonomie vom geschichtlichen Standpunkte*, iii. § 3.

which are due to the indefatigable research and the scientific fertility of the German intellect, I am quite unable to discover what other scientific treatment of the general theory of distribution and exchange they propose to substitute for the treatment which they sweepingly criticise. I cannot perceive that their higher view of man as a moral, sympathetic, public-spirited being, habitually rising above the sordid huckstering considerations by which English economists assume him to be governed, has any material effect on their theory of the determination of economic quantities when it comes to be actually worked out. When Knies[1], for instance, is discussing the nature and functions of capital, money, and credit, or when he is arguing with more subtlety than success against the Ricardian doctrine of rent, we find that the capitalists and landlords, the lenders and borrowers, whose operations are contemplated, exhibit throughout the familiar features of the old economic man. So, again, when, in the Encyclopædia

[1] See his *Geld und Credit*—in particular, *Credit*, pt. ii. ch. xii. § 2.

of Political Economy[1] recently published by this
school, we examine the definitions of fundamental
notions, or the explanation of prices, or the theory of
distribution, we meet, indeed, with some interesting
variations on the old doctrines, but we find everywhere the old economic motives assumed and the
old method unhesitatingly applied. The proof of
the pudding, as the proverb says, is in the eating;
but our historical friends make no attempt to set
before us the new economic pudding which their
large phrases seemed to promise. It is only the old
pudding with a little more ethical sauce and a little
more garnish of historical illustrations.

In saying this I should be sorry to seem to
underrate the debt that economic science owes to
the labours of the school now dominant in Germany.
Much of the positive work that they have produced
is in its way excellent; even their criticism of the
older method has been, in my opinion, most useful;
and if I complain that they have by no means done
what they announced, with some flourish of trumpets,

[1] See Schönberg's *Handbuch*, iv. v. and xi.

that they were going to do, it is chiefly because
their exaggerated phrases have led critics of a looser
sort to misunderstand and misrepresent the recent
progress and actual condition of economic thought.
I fully recognise that the elaborate and careful study
of economic facts in all departments, which the
historical school has encouraged and carried out, is
an indispensable aid to the due development of
general economic theory. In all abstract economic
reasoning which aims at quantitative precision, there
is necessarily a hypothetical element; the facts to
which the reasonings relate are not contemplated
in their actual complexity, but in an artificially
simplified form; if, therefore, the reasoning is not
accompanied and checked by a careful study of facts,
the required simplification may easily go too far or
be inappropriate in kind, so that the hypothetical
element of the reasoning is increased to an extent
which prevents the result from having any practical
value. And this danger is enhanced by the great,
though generally gradual, changes in economic
facts which accompany or constitute industrial

development. Thus, for instance, a theoretical investigation of the purchasing power of money, which assumes for simplicity that coin and bank-notes form the sole medium of exchange, might easily lead to serious practical errors in the existing condition of industry; and a theory of capital which ignores the great and growing preponderance of auxiliary over remuneratory capital is liable to be similarly delusive. The general study of economic history is important as calling attention to this source of error; but for effective protection against it we must look to that patient and systematic development of statistical inquiry, which it is one of our main functions here to watch and to foster.

I must observe, however, that the historical economists are apt to insist too onesidedly on the progress in economic theory attained by studying the industrial organisation of society in different stages of its development; they do not sufficiently recognise that other kind of progress which consists in conceiving more clearly, accurately, and consistently, the fundamental facts that remain without material change. But this latter kind of progress is very palpable to one who traces back the history of economic doctrines. Indeed, if our active controversy on principles and method has led anyone to think that political economists are always wrangling, and never establishing anything, he may easily correct this impression by turning to the older writers, and noting the confusions they make on points that are now clear to all instructed persons, and the inferences they unhesitatingly draw, which all would now admit to be in whole or in part erroneous. And by the 'older writers' I do not mean merely those who lived before Adam Smith : what I have just said is no less true of the *Wealth of Nations* and its most distinguished successors. A tiro can now see the fallacy of Adam Smith's statement, that 'labour never varying in its own value' is a 'universal' and 'accurate standard of the exchangeable value of all commodities at all times and places'; the staunchest Ricardian would refuse to follow his master in maintaining that a tax on

corn would cause labourers 'no other inconvenience
than that which they would suffer from any other
mode of taxation'; the most faithful disciple of
J. S. Mill would not fall into the confusion between
'interest' and 'profit' which seriously impairs the
value of important parts of his discussions. Much
progress, I doubt not, still remains to be made, by
steadily continuing that labour of reflective analysis
through which our conception of fundamental
economic facts has grown continually fuller and
more exact ; but no one who examines impartially
the writings of our most eminent predecessors can
ignore the progress that has already been made.

I now pass to consider another old charge against
political economists, which has been recently revived :
the charge of confining their attention too much to
the special group of phenomena with which they are
primarily concerned, and neglecting the relations of
these to other social facts. There have, no doubt,
been writers—Senior is, perhaps, the most important—in whom such neglect was deliberate and
systematic; but their peculiar view of economic

method has long ceased to have much influence on current thought; and I hardly think that political economists are now more open to the charge of systematic narrowness than any other set of students who do not 'take all knowledge for their province,' but accept the limitations which the present state of research imposes as the inevitable condition of thorough work in any department. And so far as the charge hits a real defect, I doubt whether vague generalities about the 'consensus of the different functions of the social organism,' and the impossibility of 'isolating the study of one organ from that of the rest,' will be found of much practical use in correcting the defect; since the relations of other social phenomena to those which primarily concern the economist vary indefinitely in closeness and importance; so that the question how far it is needful to investigate them is one which has to be answered very differently in relation to different economic inquiries. Thus, in considering generally the first subject of Adam Smith's investigation—'the causes of the improvement in the productive powers of labour'—the importance of a healthy condition of social morality must not be overlooked; but it is not therefore the economist's duty to study in detail the doctrine or discipline of the different Christian churches: while any reference he may make to the history of the Fine Arts will obviously be still more remote and brief. If, however, we are considering historically the causes that have affected the interest of capital, the views of Christian theologians with regard to usury will require careful attention; if, again, we are investigating the share taken by a particular community in the international organisation of industry, the higher average of artistic sensibility among its members may be a consideration deserving of notice—as in the case of France.

Or again, we may illustrate the different degrees in which economic science is connected with different departments of social fact by comparing the chief classes of statistics with which it has been our custom here to deal. Some of the most important of these—such as the statistics of taxation, trade, railways, land-tenure and the like, and a great part of the statistics of population—supply the indispensable premisses of much of the economist's reasoning, so far as it aims at being precise and particular, and the indispensable verification of many of his conclusions. In other cases again,—as, for instance, the great departments of sanitary and educational statistics,—the interest of the economist is more general and limited : for though both sanitation and education have important bearings on the productiveness of national labour, the details of the organisation for promoting either end lie in the main beyond the scope of his investigation ; while he has manifestly still less to do with criminal statistics, military and naval statistics, and several other species of social facts which governmental or private agencies now enable us to ascertain with approximate quantitative exactness.

At this point, however, our critics will probably say that it is not so much a knowledge of the separate relations of different groups of social phenomena that the political economist lacks, but rather a true conception of the social organism as a whole,

and of the fundamental laws of its development;
he does not recognise that his study can only be
legitimately or profitably pursued as a duly subordi-
nated branch of the general science of sociology.
This view was strongly urged by Mr Ingram in his
presidential address to this Section seven years ago
in Dublin[1]; and it was enforced by pointing con-
temptuously to the limited function which well-in-
structed economists at the present day are careful to
allot to their science in the settlement of practical
questions. When we explain, with Cairnes, that
political economy furnishes certain data that go
towards the formation of a sound opinion on such
questions, but does not undertake to pronounce a
final judgment on them, we are told that this 'systematic indifferentism amounts to an entire paralysis
of political economy as a social power'; and that the
time has come for it to make way for, or be absorbed
into, the 'scientific sociology' which is now in the

---

[1] It has been recently expressed again, with no less emphasis,
in Mr Ingram's article on 'Political Economy,' in the nineteenth
volume of the *Encyclopædia Britannica*.

field, and which certainly seems ready to offer statesmen the dogmatic, comprehensive, and complete
practical guidance that mere economic science con-
fesses itself inadequate to supply.

It appears to me that Mr Ingram and his friends
somewhat mistake the point that they have to prove.
It is not necessary to show that if we could ascertain
from the past history of human society the fundamental laws of social evolution as a whole, so that
we could accurately forecast the main features of the
future state with which our present social world is
pregnant—it is not needful, I say, to show that the
science which gave this foresight would be of the
highest value to a statesman, and would absorb or
dominate our present political economy. What has
to be proved is that this supremely important knowledge is within our grasp; that the sociology which
professes this prevision is really an established science.
To deny this may perhaps seem presumptuous, in
view of the voluminous works that we possess on
the subject, which it would be quite out of place
for me to attempt to criticise methodically on the

present occasion. Fortunately, however, such methodical criticism is not required to justify my negative conclusion : since there are two simple tests of the real establishment of a science—emphatically recognised by Comte in his discussion of this very subject—which can be quickly and decisively applied to the claims of existing sociology. These tests may be characterised as (1) Consensus or Continuity and (2) Prevision. The former I will explain in Comte's own words :—' When we find that recent works, instead of being the result and development of what has gone before, have a character as personal as that of their authors, and bring the most fundamental ideas into question '— then, says Comte, we may be sure we are not dealing with any doctrine deserving the name of positive science. Now, if we compare the most elaborate and ambitious treatises on sociology, of which there happens to be one in each of the three leading scientific languages—Comte's *Politique Positive*, Spencer's *Sociology*, and Schäffle's *Bau und Leben des socialen Körpers*,—we see at once that they exhibit the most complete and conspicuous absence of agreement or continuity in their treatment of the fundamental questions of social evolution.

Take, for example, the question of the future of religion. No thoughtful person can overlook the importance of religion as an element of man's social existence; nor do the sociologists to whom I have referred fail to recognise it. But if we inquire after the characteristics of the religion of which their science leads them to foresee the coming prevalence, they give with nearly equal confidence answers as divergent as can be conceived. Schäffle cannot comprehend that the place of the great Christian Churches can be taken by anything but a purified form of Christianity; Spencer contemplates complacently the reduction of religious thought and sentiment to a perfectly indefinite consciousness of an Unknowable and the emotion that accompanies this peculiar intellectual exercise; while Comte has no doubt that the whole history of religion—which, as he says, 'should resume the entire history of human development'—has been leading up to the worship of the Great Being, Humanity, personified domestically for each normal male individual by his nearest female relatives. It would certainly seem that the science which allows these discrepancies in its chief expositors must be still in its infancy. And when we go on to ask how these divergent forecasts of the future are scientifically deduced from the study of the past evolution of mankind, we are irresistibly reminded of the old epigram as to the relation of certain theological controversialists to the Bible:

Hic liber est in quo quærit sua dogmata quisque,
     Invenit et pariter dogmata quisque sua.

I do not doubt that our sociologists are sincere in setting before us their conception of the coming social state as the last term of a series of which the law has been discovered by patient historical study; but when we look closely into their work it becomes only too evident that each philosopher has constructed on the basis of personal feeling and experience his ideal future in which our present social deficiencies are to be remedied; and that the process by which history is arranged in steps pointing towards his Utopia bears not the faintest resemblance to a scientific demonstration.

This is equally evident when we turn from religion to industry, and examine the forecasts of industrial development offered to the statesman in the name of scientific sociology as a substitute for the discarded calculations of the mere economist. With equal confidence, history is represented as leading up, now to the naïve and unqualified individualism of Spencer, now to the carefully guarded and elaborated socialism of Schäffle, now to Comte's dream of securing seven-roomed houses for all working men—with other comforts to correspond—solely by the impressive moral precepts of his philosophic priests. Guidance, truly, is here enough and to spare : but how is the bewildered statesman to select his guidance when his sociological doctors exhibit this portentous disagreement ?

Nor is it only that they adopt diametrically opposite conclusions : we find that each adopts his conclusion with the most serene and complete indifference to the line of historical reasoning on which his brother sociologist relies. Schäffle, *e.g.*, appears not to have the least inkling of the array of facts which have convinced Spencer that the recent movement towards increased industrial intervention of government in Germany and England is causally connected with the contemporaneous recrudescence of 'militancy' in the two countries. And similarly, when Spencer explains how, under a régime of private property and free contract, there is necessarily a 'correct apportioning of reward to merit,' so that each worker 'obtains as much benefit as his efforts are equivalent to—no more and no less,' he exhibits a total ignorance of the crushing refutation which, according to Schäffle, this individualistic fallacy has received at the hands of socialism. The tendency of free competition to annihilate itself, and give birth to monopolies exercised against the common interest for the private advantage of the monopolists; the crushing inequality of industrial opportunities, which the legal equality and freedom of modern society has no apparent tendency to correct; the impossibility of remunerating by private sale of commodities some

most important services to the community; the un-
foreseen fluctuations of supply and demand which a
world-wide organisation of industry brings with it,
liable to inflict, to an increasing extent, undeserved
economic ruin upon large groups of industrious
workers; the waste incident to the competitive
system, through profuse and ostentatious advertise-
ments, needless multiplication of middle-men, inevitable non-employment, or half-employment, of
many competitors; the demoralisation, worse than
waste, due to the reckless or fraudulent promotion of
joint-stock companies, and to the gambling rife in
the great markets, and tending more and more to
spread over the whole area of production—such
points as these are unnoticed in the broad view
which our English sociologist takes of the modern
industrial society gradually emancipating itself from
militancy: it never enters his head that they can have
anything to do with causing the movement towards
socialism to which his German *confrère* has yielded[1].

---

[1] See Schäffle's 'Kritik der kapitalistischen Epoche,' in *Bau
und Leben des socialen Körpers*, vol. iii. pp. 419—457.

However, whether Spencer or Schäffle is a true prophet—whether the decay of war will bring us to a more complete individualism, or whether the increasing scale of the organisation of industry and its increasingly marked deficiencies are preparing the way for socialism—cannot certainly be known before a date more or less distant. But as Comte's sociological treatise was written a generation ago, we are fortunately able to bring his very definite predictions and counsels to the test of accomplished facts. In 1854 he announced that the transition which was to terminate the Western Revolution, would be organised from Paris, the 'religious metropolis of regenerate humanity,' where an 'irreversible dictatorship' had just been established, within the space of a generation. In the initial phase of the transition, which ought to last about seven years, perfect freedom of the press would 'rapidly extinguish journalism,' owing to the 'inability of the journal to compete with the placard.' By a 'judicious use of placards, with a few occasional pamphlets,' Positivism would regenerate public opinion. The budget of the clergy, the University of France, the Academy of Sciences must be suppressed, and the proximate abolition of copyright announced. By these moderate measures Louis Napoleon's irreversible dictatorship might be 'perfected and consolidated,' so that the dictator might assume complete legislative power, reducing the Representative Assembly—which would sit once in three years—to the purely financial function of voting the budget. In the second phase of the transition, which should last about five years, the 'dictatorial government now unquestionably progressive,' would suppress the French army, substituting a constabulary of 80,000 gendarmes. This would suffice to maintain order, internal and external, as the oppressive military establishments of neighbouring states would everywhere fall as soon as France had put down her army. The dictator would then break up France into seventeen separate intendancies, as a step towards the ultimate Positive régime, under which the peoples of Western Europe are to be distributed into seventy republics, comprising about 300,000 families each. The third and last phase of the transition, which should occupy about twenty-one years, might be expected to be opened by the voluntary abdication of the dictator in favour of a triumvirate, consisting probably of a banker to manage foreign affairs, an 'agricultural patrician' as minister of the interior, and a working man to take charge of the finances. Their names would be suggested by the High Priest of Humanity —indeed, Comte tells us that he had been 'working for several years at the choice of persons,' in order to be ready for this momentous nomination: for the immense influence which Positivist doctrine ought to have gained by this time would enable the political direction of France to be placed completely in the hands of Positivists. This triumvirate would transform the seventeen intendancies into separate republics: the *bourgeoisie* would then be gradually 'eliminated' by the extinction of *littérateurs*, lawyers, and small capitalists, so that society would pass easily into the final régime[1].

[1] These details are taken from Comte's *Système de Politique Positive*, vol. iv. chap. v.

I need not go on to this final régime : I have already given you more than enough of these extravagances; but it seemed important to show how completely the delusive belief that he had constructed the science of sociology could transform a philosopher of remarkable power and insight into the likeness of a crazy charlatan. I trust that our Association will take no step calculated to foster delusions of this kind. There is no reason to despair of the progress of general sociology; but I do not think that its development can be really promoted by shutting our eyes to its present very rudimentary condition. When the general science of society has solved the problems which it has as yet only managed to define more or less clearly—when for positive knowledge it can offer us something better than a mixture of vague and variously applied physiological analogies, imperfectly verified historical generalisations, and unwarranted political predictions—when it has succeeded in establishing on the basis of a really scientific induction its forecasts of social evolution—it will not require any formal admission to the discussions of this Section; its existence will be irresistibly felt throughout the range of the more special inquiries into different departments of social fact to which we have hitherto restricted ourselves. It is our business in the meantime to carry on our more limited and empirical studies of society in as scientific a manner as possible. Of the method of statistical investigation I have not presumed to speak, as I have not myself done any work of this kind, but have merely availed myself gratefully of the labours of others. But, even so, it has been impossible for me not to learn that to do this work in its entirety, as it ought to be done, requires scientific faculties of a high order. For duly discerning the various sources of error that impede the quantitative ascertainment of social facts, eliminating such error as far as possible, and allowing for it where it cannot be eliminated—still more for duly analysing differences and fluctuations in the social quantities ascertained, and distinguishing causal from accidental variations and correspondences—there is needed not only industry, patience, accuracy, but a perpetually alert and circumspect activity of the reasoning powers; nor is the statistician completely equipped for his task of discovering empirical laws unless he can effectively use the assistance of an abstract and difficult calculus of probabilities. It is satisfactory to think that there is every prospect of statistical investigations being carried on, in an increasingly comprehensive and systematic manner, throughout an ever widening range of civilised countries. The results of this development cannot fail to be important from the statesman's no less than the theorist's point of view: for though the statistician, as such, does not profess to guide public opinion on political questions, there can be no doubt—as Mc.Giffen has recently pointed out—that the knowledge attained by him tends to exercise on the general discussion of such questions an influence, on the whole, no less salutary than profound.

Cambridge:

PRINTED BY C. J. CLAY, M.A. & SON,

AT THE UNIVERSITY PRESS.

MESSRS. MACMILLAN AND CO.'S PUBLICATIONS.

By the same Author.

THE METHODS OF ETHICS. Third Edition, revised throughout, with Important Additions. 8vo. 14s.

A Supplement to the Second Edition, containing all the important Additions and Alterations in the Third Edition. Demy 8vo. 6s.

"Full of interesting matter, treated with judicial impartiality."
— *Saturday Review.*

THE PRINCIPLES OF POLITICAL ECONOMY. 8vo. 16s.

"Mr. Sidgwick has given us many able discussions, in which cases are summed up and judgment given, when it is given, in a judicial spirit and a luminous manner. It is unquestionably the weightiest book on the subject which has appeared in this country for some time....It deserves to be carefully studied by all whose interest in political economy is not merely superficial." — *Academy.*

"We believe we are not exaggerating when we say it is the expectation, among men well able to judge, that this work will take the first place as the authority on political economy....He has discarded none of the old authorities, but he has thrown upon their generalizations some fresh light, because he has carefully observed the new forces and relations of facts which are available in these nineteenth-century times." — *British Quarterly Review.*

By Right Hon. HENRY FAWCETT, M.P., F.R.S.,
late Professor of Political Economy in the University of Cambridge.

A MANUAL OF POLITICAL ECONOMY. Sixth Edition, revised, with a chapter on "State Socialism and the Nationalisation of the Land," and an Index. Crown 8vo. 12s.

SPEECHES ON SOME CURRENT POLITICAL QUESTIONS. 8vo. 10s. 6d.

Contents :—Indian Finance—The Birmingham League—Nine Hours Bill—Election Expenses—Women's Suffrage—Household Suffrage in Counties—Irish University Education, &c.

FREE TRADE AND PROTECTION. An enquiry into the Causes which have retarded the general adoption of Free Trade since its Introduction into England. New and Cheaper Edition. Crown 8vo. 3s. 6d.

INDIAN FINANCE. Three Essays. With Introduction and Appendix. 8vo. 7s. 6d.

By MILLICENT GARRETT FAWCETT.

POLITICAL ECONOMY FOR BEGINNERS, WITH QUESTIONS. Fourth Edition. 18mo. 2s. 6d.

TALES IN POLITICAL ECONOMY. Crown 8vo. 3s.

ESSAYS AND LECTURES ON POLITICAL AND SOCIAL SUBJECTS. By Right Hon. HENRY FAWCETT, M.P., F.R.S. and MILLICENT GARRETT FAWCETT. 8vo. 10s. 6d.

MACMILLAN & CO., LONDON.

MESSRS. MACMILLAN AND CO.'S PUBLICATIONS.

By ALFRED MARSHALL, M.A.

THE PRESENT POSITION OF ECONOMICS. An Inaugural Lecture given in the Senate House at Cambridge on February 24, 1885. By ALFRED MARSHALL, M.A., Professor of Political Economy in the University of Cambridge; late Fellow of Balliol College, Oxford, &c. Crown 8vo. 2s.

THE ECONOMICS OF INDUSTRY. By ALFRED MARSHALL, M.A., Professor of Political Economy in the University of Cambridge, &c., and MARY PALEY MARSHALL, late Lecturer at Newnham Hall, Cambridge. Extra fcap. 8vo. 2s. 6d.

By W. STANLEY JEVONS, LL.D., M.A., F.R.S.

INVESTIGATIONS IN CURRENCY AND FINANCE. Illustrated by Twenty Diagrams. Edited, with an Introduction, by H. S. FOXWELL, M.A., Fellow and Lecturer of St John's College, Cambridge, and Professor of Political Economy at University College, London. Demy 8vo. 21s.

METHODS OF SOCIAL REFORM. Demy 8vo. 10s. 6d.

THE PRINCIPLES OF SCIENCE: A TREATISE ON LOGIC AND SCIENTIFIC METHOD. New and Cheaper Edition, revised. Crown 8vo. 12s. 6d.

THE THEORY OF POLITICAL ECONOMY. Second Edition, revised and enlarged, with New Preface, &c. 8vo. 10s. 6d.

STUDIES IN DEDUCTIVE LOGIC. A Manual for Students. Second Edition. Crown 8vo. 6s.

By FRANCIS A. WALKER, M.A., Ph.D.,
Professor of Political Economy and History, Sheffield Scientific School of Yale College; late Chief of the U.S. Bureau of Statistics, &c. &c.

THE WAGES QUESTION. A treatise on Wages and the Wages Class. 8vo. 14s.

MONEY. 8vo. 16s.

MONEY IN ITS RELATION TO TRADE AND INDUSTRY. Crown 8vo. 7s. 6d.

POLITICAL ECONOMY. 8vo. 10s. 6d.

LAND AND ITS RENT. Fcap. 8vo. 3s. 6d.

By DR LUIGI COSSA,
Professor in the University of Pavia.

GUIDE TO THE STUDY OF POLITICAL ECONOMY. Translated from the Second Italian Edition. With a Preface by W. STANLEY JEVONS, F.R.S. Crown 8vo. 4s. 6d.

MACMILLAN AND CO., LONDON.

UNIVERSITY OF TORONTO
LIBRARY

—

Do not

remove

the card

from this

Pocket.

—

Acme Library Card Pocket
Under Pat. "Ref. Index File."
Made by LIBRARY BUREAU

www.ingramcontent.com/pod-product-compliance
Lightning Source LLC
Chambersburg PA
CBHW031245260626
47169CB00007B/2455